HOW TO MAKE YOUR OWN KN...

How to
Make your own kinetics

David Wickers
and Sharon Finmark

STUDIO VISTA London

 VAN NOSTRAND REINHOLD COMPANY New York

A Studio Vista/Van Nostrand Reinhold How-to Book

Text and drawings copyright © 1972 by David Wickers and Sharon Finmark
Photographs © 1972 by Studio Vista

Photoset, printed and bound in England by
BAS Printers Limited, Wallop, Hampshire

Published in Great Britain by
Studio Vista
Blue Star House, Highgate Hill, London N19
and in the United States by
Van Nostrand Reinhold Company
A Division of Litton Educational Publishing, Inc.
450 West 33rd Street, New York, N.Y. 10001.

Library of Congress Catalog Card Number 79–161978
ISBN 0 289 70219 4

Contents

Introduction

The world in which we live is full of moving objects of one kind or another. Motor cars are driven along our streets, birds fly overhead, the television brings moving pictures to our homes.

This book is also about moving objects. If you paint a picture or make a clay model it will stay exactly the same once it is finished. But Kinetic Art is much more exciting. Kinetics change all the time as you watch them or play with them and they seem almost to come alive.

You do not need expensive motors or complicated electrical power to make Kinetics work. By using such everyday objects as coloured paper, oil, water, mirrors, beads, magnets and plastic bags you can easily make your own moving world.

Flowering spiral

You need:
white card
compasses
a thick, black felt marker
a sheet of acetate or thick cellophane
scissors
ruler
pencil
drawing-pin (thumbtack)

1 Draw a large circle on the card, making the radius at least 12 cm. (5 in.). Keep the compasses set at the same radius and put the point anywhere on the edge of the circle. Draw a curve from the edge of the circle to the centre.

2 Put the point of the compasses where this curve touches the edge of the circle and draw another curve to the centre. Repeat this all the way round the circle.

3 Put the point of the compasses on the edge of the circle half way between two of the curves. Continue round the circle in the same way as before. Repeat this until you have drawn 24 curves.

4 Blacken and thicken the lines with a felt marker.

5 Draw on the acetate a circle with the same radius as the first one. Keeping the point of the compasses where it is, draw a second, larger circle on the acetate. Lay the acetate over the card and mark on it the 24 points where the curves touch the edge of the smaller circle. With the felt marker draw a straight line from each point to the centre of the acetate circle.

6 Cut round the edge of the card circle and round the larger acetate circle. Lay the acetate on the card. Push a drawing-pin through the centre of both circles and pin them to the wall. Turn the acetate slowly round and round.

The two sets of lines will move like a never-ending spiral when you rotate the top sheet. This is a moiré.

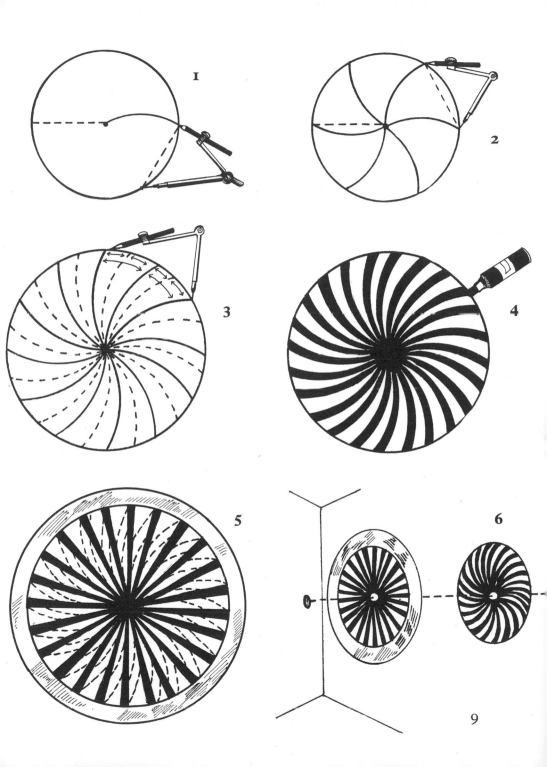

I

2

3

4

5

6

9

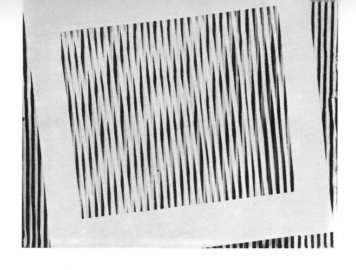

Prison bars

You need:
corrugated cardboard
a piece of white card
ruler and pencil
needle and cotton
glue
drawing-pins
scissors
black and white paint

1 Paint the corrugated cardboard white. When it is dry, paint the raised stripes black (or use a broad felt-tipped pen instead).

2 Draw lines on the white card the same distance apart as the width of the stripes on the corrugated cardboard.

3 Cut a strip off the bottom of the card and put it on one side.

4 Cut along the lines you have drawn, leaving a margin on all three sides. Cut across the top of alternate stripes and remove them completely. Take the piece of card you set aside and glue it to the bottoms of the strips that are left. This will make the fourth side of a frame.

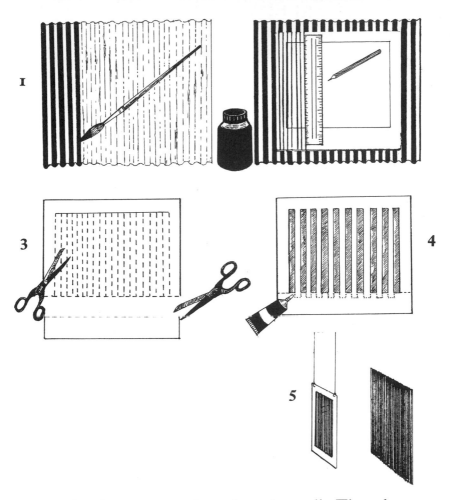

5 Pin the corrugated card to the wall. Thread some cotton through the two top corners of the card frame and hang it from the ceiling with drawing-pins. It should hang about 30 cm. (or 12 in.) in front of the corrugated card and be tilted to one side.

As you walk past the 'prison bars' their effect on your eyes may make you feel a little dizzy. It is another moiré. You can discover similar vibrating effects by laying pieces of metal gauze or net curtains on top of each other and watching the patterns that form when you move or turn them.

Film show

You need:
2 round cardboard cake
  stands
a large nail
a large bead
thin card
black paint
felt-tipped pens
scissors
roll of narrow gummed
  paper
drawing-pins
ruler

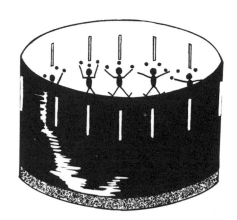

1 Cut a piece of card 15 cm. (or 6 in.) wide and long enough to wrap once around a cake stand. (You may have to join two pieces of card together.) Cut 12 evenly spaced slits in the card. They should be 6.5 cm. (or $2\frac{1}{2}$ in.) deep and 50 mm. (just under $\frac{1}{4}$ in.) wide.

2 Stick a strip of gummed paper all along the top of the slits and paint one side of the card black.

3 On the other side of the card draw your 'filmstar' in 12 different but connected positions. One figure should come directly beneath each slit. Do not let them come right to the bottom of the card. Try drawing a juggler tossing balls into the air.

4 Pin the card round the edge of one cake stand so that the figures face inwards. Find the centre point of the second cake stand by balancing it on the point of the nail. Push the nail right through and thread the bead

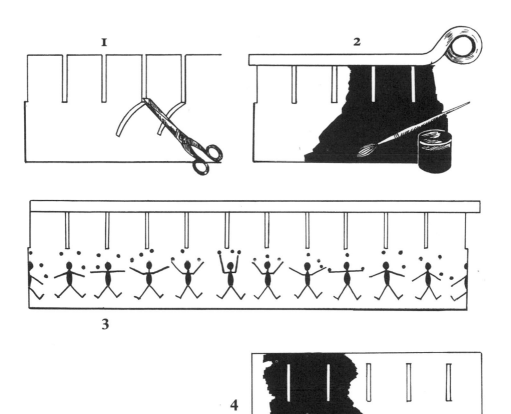

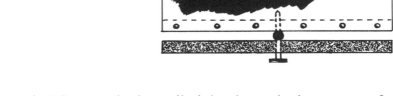

onto it. Now push the nail right through the centre of the first cake stand.

When you spin the 'film show' round and look through the slits, the juggler will seem to be tossing the balls into the air. Try drawing other film shows in the same way.

Magic pendulum
You need:
a rectangular piece of
   white card
red cellophane paper
needle and cotton
adhesive tape
crayons
drawing-pins

1 Cut a frame from around the edge of the card and put it to one side.

2 Draw a vase on the remaining part of the card using any colour except red. Now add some flowers in red crayon. (The shade of red should be the same as that of the red cellophane.)

3 Tightly cover the card frame with red cellophane and stick it down with adhesive tape. Using the needle

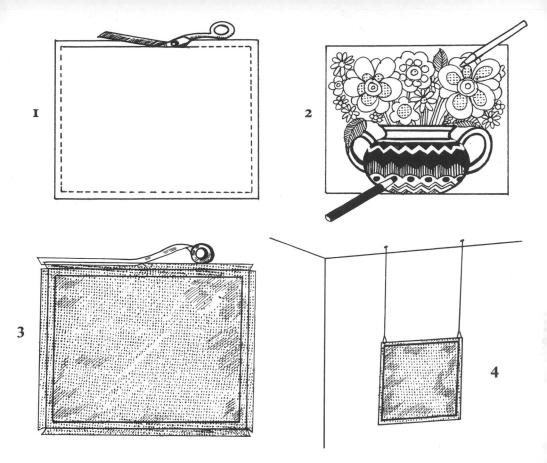

to help you, thread a length of cotton through each of the two top corners of the frame. Tie the cotton firmly to the card. Pin the other ends of the cotton to the ceiling so that the frame hangs close to the wall.

4 Pin the picture to the wall directly behind the red cellophane frame.

Start the 'pendulum' frame swaying, and you won't believe your own eyes. The flowers will disappear completely when the red cellophane passes over the picture! You could make other trick pictures in this way—a man with a red dog, perhaps, a street with a red bus, or Santa Claus sitting on a heap of toys.

Unidentified flying objects

You need:
8 'flat' magnets (not the
  horseshoe type)
thin fishing line or cotton
8 empty household
  containers (4 small,
  4 medium-sized)
a large cardboard box
a piece of fabric
coloured paper or paint
glue
scissors
matches

1 Arrange the magnets in pairs. Mark those sides that repel or push each other away when held together.

2 Glue each of the magnets on top of a container so that the marked sides face upwards.

3 Cut out one large side of the box. Glue the four largest containers to the base.

4 Attach a piece of fishing line about 60 cm. (or 24 in.) long to each of the small containers. Do this by removing the lid, making a hole in the centre with a needle, threading the fishing line through, and knotting the end round a piece of matchstick. Replace the lid.

5 Hang the small containers to the 'roof' of the box by making four small holes and attaching the fishing line in the same way as before. The magnets on the small containers should hang right above those on the larger

16

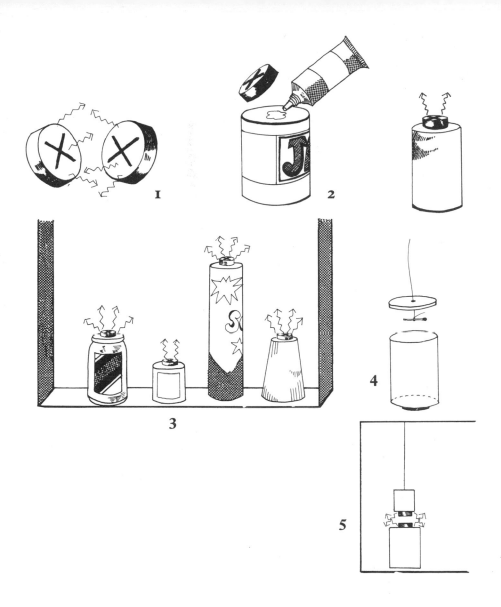

ones. The pair of magnets should come as near as possible without touching.

Hide the containers by laying the piece of fabric over them. The U.F.O.'s will hover above the ground in a very mysterious way, just like space craft.

Magnetic maze
You need:
the lid of a large cardboard
    box
iron filings
a strong magnet
strips of balsa wood
scissors
adhesive tape
4 cotton reels or spools
cellophane paper
paint

1 Paint the inside of the lid a bright colour. When it is dry, glue strips of balsa wood onto the inside of the lid at all kinds of angles to each other.

2 Glue a cotton reel or spool to each of the four corners of the other side of the lid.

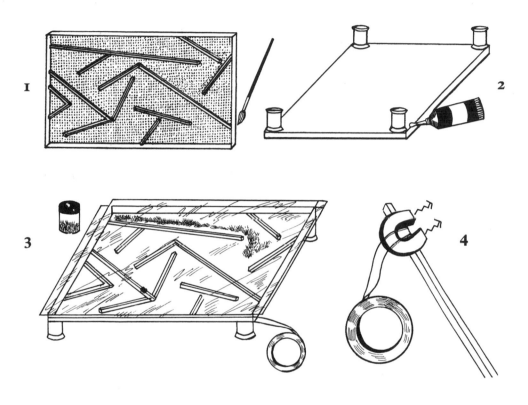

3 Put some iron filings in the lid and cover it with a sheet of cellophane paper. Stick the paper to the edges of the lid with adhesive tape.

4 Attach the magnet to a fairly thick strip of balsa wood by binding it to the end with adhesive tape.

Move the magnet around underneath the lid. You will find that the iron filings will be attracted to the magnet and follow it through the maze like an army of live insects on the march.

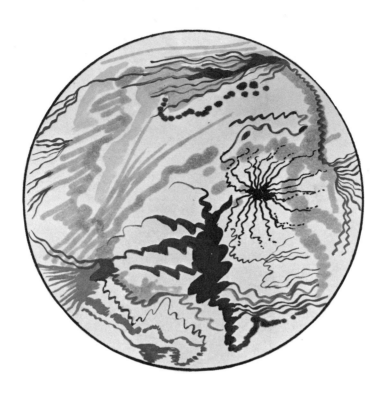

Exploding colours
You need:
artificial food dyes
large pan or dish
washing-up liquid
   (liquid detergent)
milk

1 Pour some milk into the dish. It should be about 1.5 cm. (or $\frac{1}{2}$ in.) deep.

2 Sprinkle a few drops of different coloured food dyes gently on the surface of the milk. You could use coloured inks instead, but the effect will not be as good.

1   2

3 Carefully let a drop of the liquid detergent run down
the side of the dish. It will sink beneath the surface of
the milk.

3

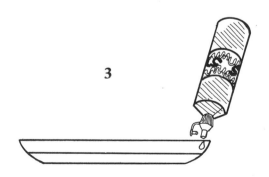

After a short while the detergent will make the colours
move around in all directions. This swirling effect will
last several minutes, forming many beautiful patterns.
You can change the direction of the movements by
adding more detergent to the other side of the dish.

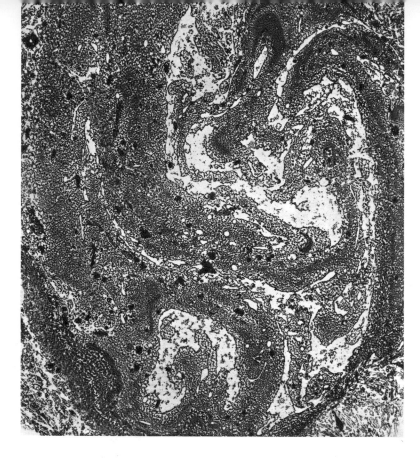

Instant print
You need:
a large, shallow dish
either: coloured waterproof
    inks
or: oil paints and
    turpentine
paper

1 Fill the dish with water. Sprinkle some drops of
coloured inks on the surface of the water. (If you use
oil paints you will have to thin them down with
turpentine.) Let the colours swirl around and, if
necessary, give them a gentle push with a pencil to
make them form spidery patterns.

2 Carefully lay a piece of paper on the surface of the water for a few seconds. Remove it just as carefully, turn it upright, and leave it to dry.

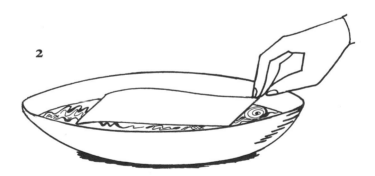

When the print is dry you will have made a lasting copy of the pattern you saw moving about on the surface of the water. You can make many more 'instant' prints by changing the types and amounts of the colours you use and the patterns they make on the water.

23

Action painting
You need:
a large sheet of paper
2 chairs
a broom handle (or
    bamboo cane)
small plastic bags
string
powder paint (Powder
    Tempera Color)

1 Place the two chairs back to back and tie the broom handle between them. Tie a short length of string onto the broom handle so that it hangs down in a loop. Tie another length of string to this loop a little away from the centre.

2 Mix some powder paint. When it is fairly thick pour it into a plastic bag. Tie the bag to the end of the string so that it hangs just above the ground.

24

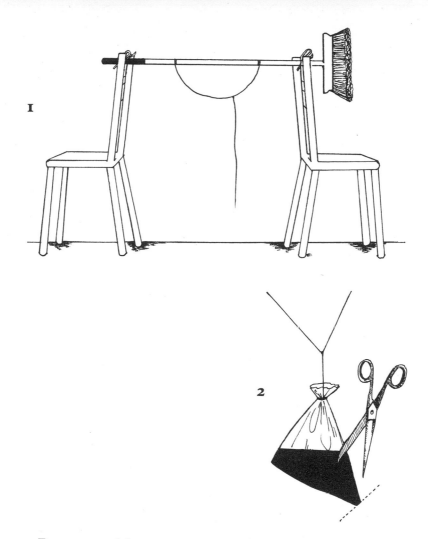

3 Put some old newspapers on the floor and then lay a large sheet of paper directly below the paint bag. Cut a small hole in one corner and set it swinging.

Although the bag is left to swing on its own, the pattern made on the paper will form a definite shape. You can also guide the movement of the bag with your hand. Use several different colours on the same sheet.

For an extra large action painting, tie the bag to a tree in the garden or to the garage roof.

Spin-a-disc
You need:
thick card
powder paints
string
pointed scissors
glue
compasses

1 Draw a circle with a radius of about 4 cm. (or $1\frac{1}{2}$ in.) on the card and cut it out.

2 Cut small triangular 'teeth' all round the edge.

3 Make two small holes in the middle of the card using the point of the compasses. Cut a small piece of card to fit in between these holes and glue it on. This will make the holes stronger.

4 Divide one side of the card into three equal areas. Paint one area bright red, another yellow, and the third blue.

5 Paint a line of coloured spots on the other side of the card. Paint a blue spot at each end of the cardboard strip, a red spot at the top edge of the card and also at the bottom edge, and a yellow spot between them.

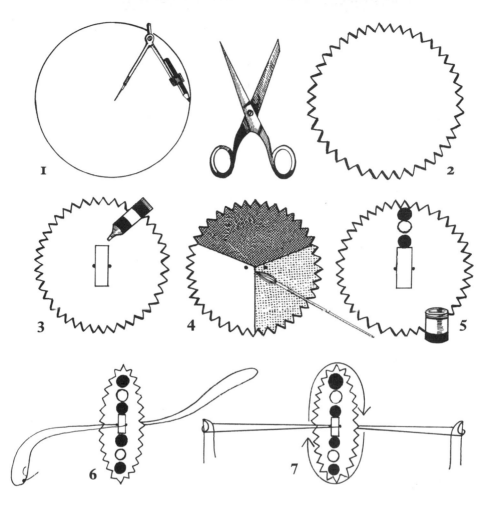

6 Thread a piece of string about 1.5 m (or 5 ft.) long through one hole and back through the other. Tie the ends together to make a loop.

7 Slip a finger through each end of the loop and wind up the spin-a-disc by twisting it round and round.

When you pull the string the spin-a-disc will whoosh through the air and wind itself up again. The spots will become rings of colour and the red, yellow and blue areas will merge to become white!

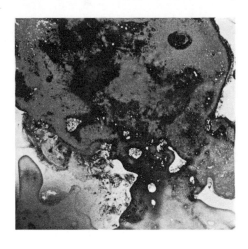

Light show
You need:
a sheet of acetate (or pieces
 of thin glass)
masking tape
Vaseline
oil paints
poster paints
turpentine
liquid paraffin
scissors

1 Cut out some pieces of acetate about 10 cm. (or 4 in.) square. If you use glass, get it cut to size in the shop.)

2 Smear some Vaseline along the edges of the squares.

3 Mix some poster paints with water and thin down the oil paints with turpentine. Put a few drops of one powder paint and a different coloured oil paint on one of the squares.

4 Lay another acetate or glass square on top of the first and seal them together round the edges with masking tape.

28

Hold the frame up to the light and bend and squeeze the two sides together. The colours will not mix, and you will see beautiful moving patterns.

If you would prefer to use just one colour, try liquid paraffin with a poster colour or water with an oil colour. You could also pour the paints and liquid into a bottle or plastic bag and watch the bubbles of colour move around.

Kaleidoscope

You need:
2 pieces of mirror about
    20 cm. × 4 cm. (or
    8½ in. × 1½ in.)
thin cardboard
coloured gummed paper
adhesive tape
small plastic bag
greaseproof paper
scissors

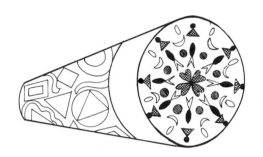

1 Place two mirrors side by side facing inwards. Join them together along the top with adhesive tape.

2 Cut a strip of cardboard 2.5 cm. (or 1 in.) wide and the same length as the mirrors. Use adhesive tape to join its long edges to the mirrors to form a triangular column.

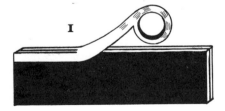

1

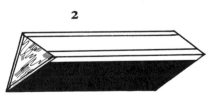

2

3 Roll a piece of cardboard into a tube around the mirrors so that they are firmly held inside. Stick it down with adhesive tape.

4 Stick a piece of plastic over one end of the tube. On the other end stick a circle of card with a peephole cut in the middle.

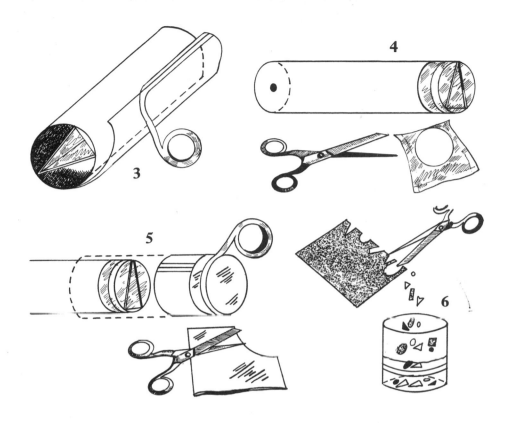

5 Wrap a piece of cardboard about 5 cm. (or 2 in.) wide tightly round the tube. Tape the ends together to make a second, shorter tube and slide it off the longer one. Stick some greaseproof paper over one end.

6 Glue some pieces of gummed paper back to back so that both sides are coloured, and cut out several small shapes. Put them inside the shorter tube. Slide this shorter tube back onto the longer one. Decorate the whole kaleidoscope with gummed paper shapes.

You will see all kinds of patterns when you turn the end of the kaleidoscope. You could experiment with small beads or sequins or other small objects instead of paper shapes.

Carousel
You need:
thick white card
coloured cellophane paper
modelling knife or pointed
    scissors
adhesive tape
cotton
drawing-pin
needle

1 Cut a large circle of card
about 45 cm. (or 18 in.)
across. Cut slits 5 cm.
(or 2 in.) long from the edge
towards the centre, spacing
them about 5 cm. apart.

(For diagrams see page 35.)

2 Cut a pattern of holes
in the circle of card.
Cover each hole with
cellophane paper stuck
down with adhesive tape.

3 Fold one edge of each of
the slits downwards to make
small flaps.

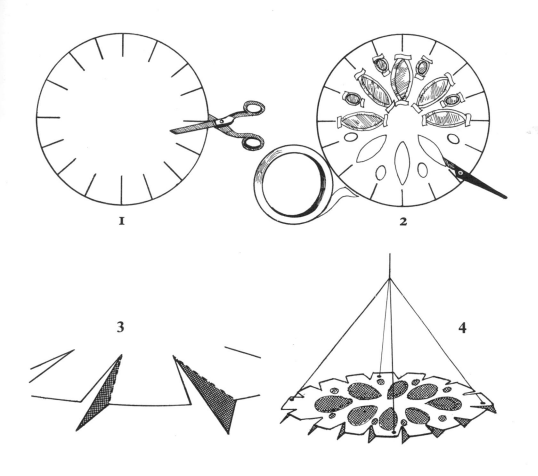

4 Make four tiny holes in the edge of the card circle. Thread cotton through them and join the ends together so that the circle hangs horizontally. Attach it to the ceiling with cotton and a drawing-pin, and place a table lamp beneath it.

At night the heat from the lamp will turn the carousel and the light will cast a brightly-coloured pattern on the ceiling.

Instructions for making this menacing wind dragon appear on page 36

C

Wind dragon
You need:
a long stick or cane
sheets of coloured tissue
    paper
galvanized wire
string
pliers
scissors
adhesive tape

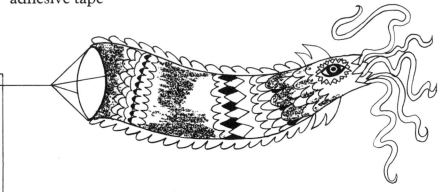

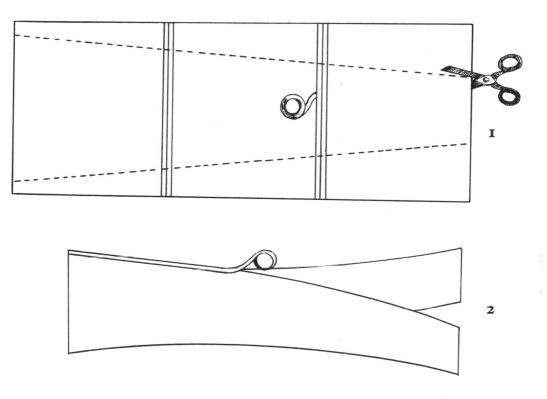

1 Join together some sheets of green tissue paper with the adhesive tape so that they form two lengths of about 1.5 m. (or 5 ft.). Trim the sides of both pieces to make them about 45 cm. (or 18 in.) wide at one end and about half that width at the other.

2 Lay one piece of tissue paper over the other and join them together by sticking adhesive tape all along the edges. Leave both ends open.

3 Cut out some rows of 'scales' from a different colour tissue paper and stick them onto the basic shape. Cut zig-zag 'jaws' in the narrower end and stick on two decorative tissue paper eyes.

4 Cut several long, thin streamers of red tissue paper and stick them to the inside of the jaws to look like flames.

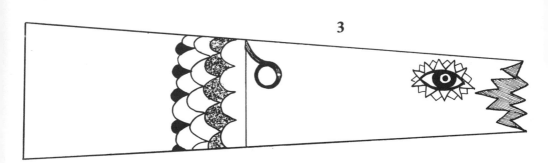

3

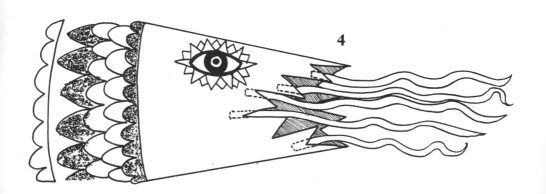

4

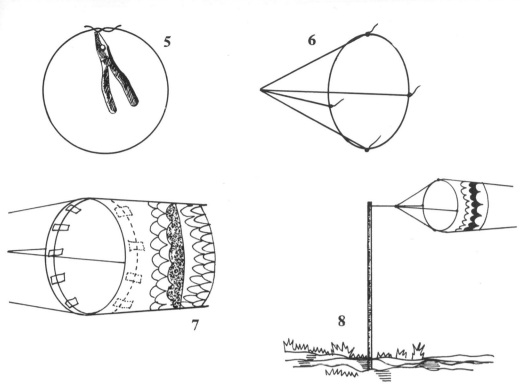

5 With the pliers cut a piece of galvanized wire about 90 cm. (or 3 ft.) long. Bend it into a circle and twist the two ends together.

6 Tie four pieces of string to the wire circle and knot their ends together.

7 Place the wire circle just inside the larger open end of the dragon and stick it to the paper with adhesive tape.

8 Push the stick or cane into some soft earth and tie a short length of string to the top. Join this to the four pieces attached to the wire.

The wind will fill the dragon's body and make it twist round in the air with flames shooting menacingly from its jaws.

Space orbit
You need:
galvanized wire
coloured card
compasses
cotton
needle
glue
pliers
scissors

1 Cut five shapes from the card to represent the sun, moon, earth, a star, and Saturn (with its rings). Make the largest about 15 cm. (or 6 in.) across and the smallest about 5 cm. (2 in.). Thread a piece of cotton through each shape as shown in the diagram.

2 Cut the wire into four lengths of 30, 40, 50 and 60 cm. (or 12, 16, 20 and 24 in.). Bend them into gently curved arms. Bend each end of each piece of wire right back to make a small hook.

3 Hang the two smallest shapes from the hooks on the shortest wire arm. Now find the point on the arm where the two shapes balance each other exactly. Tie and glue a length of cotton to this point. Join the other end of the cotton to the next longest arm. Add the next largest shape. Find the point of balance on the second arm. Continue 'balancing and attaching' until the mobile is complete.

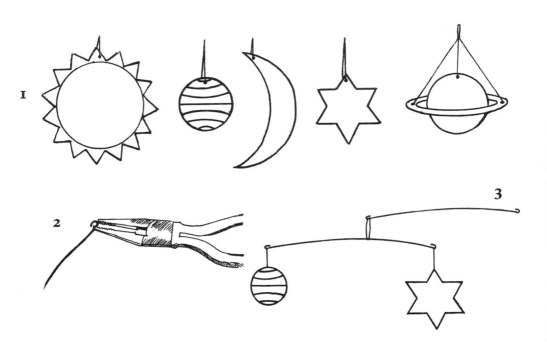

Ordinary indoor air currents will move your mobile. Hang it from the ceiling with a drawing-pin and watch the heavens revolve. You can make other mobiles using all kinds of shapes and designs.

Merry-go-round
You need:
thin coloured card
compasses
cotton
needle
drawing-pin

1 Draw a spiral on the card like this: first draw a straight line and then, from point x, draw a semi-circle on it with the compasses. Put the point of the compasses on y and draw a second semi-circle on the other side of the line, starting where the first one finished. Build up your spiral in this way, using x and y alternately as the centre point of the semi-circles.

2 Cut along the line of the spiral.

3 Thread a length of cotton through the centre of the spiral and knot the other end round a piece of matchstick. Pin the spiral to the ceiling with a drawing-pin, positioning it above a radiator.

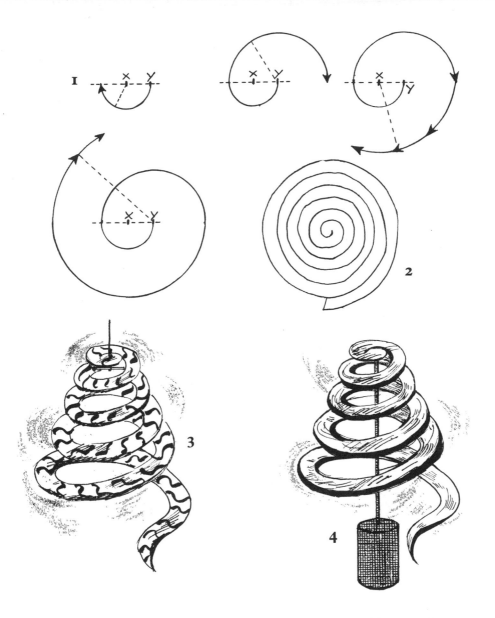

The warm currents of air from the fire will turn the
spiral round and round. You could hang several spirals
from an old hula hoop; or make much smaller ones to
fit on a knitting needle stuck in a cork (fig. 4), or on a
pencil pushed into a matchbox.

Tap dancer
You need:
3 m. (or 10 ft.) of narrow
    square balsa wood
strong glue
balsa cement
twine
5 large ball-bearings
modelling knife
dressmaking pins

1 Cut the balsa into 4 lengths of 30 cm. (or 1 ft.) and eight lengths of 20 cm. (or 8 in.). Make two rectangles by cementing two long pieces to two short pieces.

2 Cement the remaining four short pieces to the corners of one rectangle so that they stand upright. Pin them so that they stay in position.

3 Just before they set rigid, cement the other rectangular frame on the top to make a box. Pin it in position. Allow the cement to set completely.

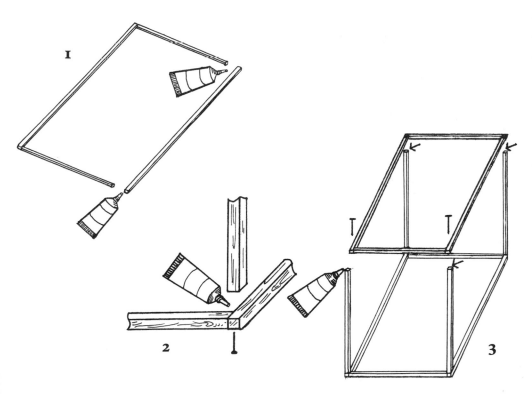

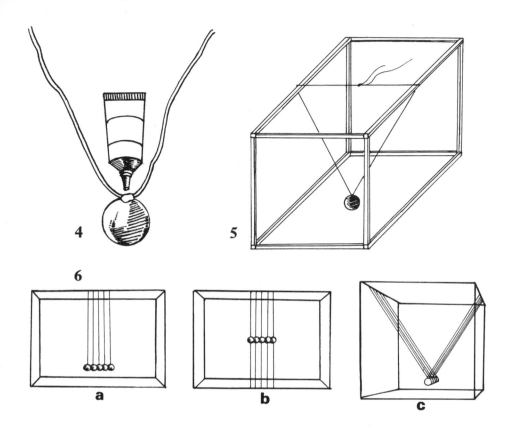

4 Cut 5 pieces of twine 60 cm. (or 2 ft.) long. Attach a ball-bearing to the middle of each piece of twine with strong glue. Leave the glue to set hard.

5 Tie the ends of the twine loosely together round the top of the frame so that the balls hang down in a 'V'.

6 Carefully adjust the knots so that the balls hang in a perfect straight line. They should hang down to exactly the same level and should just touch each other. Check this by looking along the line of the balls: a from the side, b from above, and c from one end.

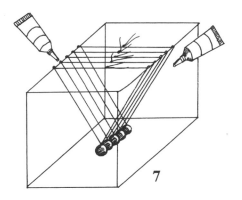
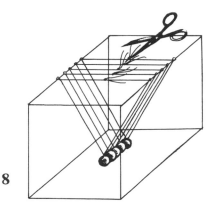

7 When the balls are properly arranged (this may take some time), glue the twine in place on the two supporting arms of the box. Be careful not to move the twine.

8 When the glue has set, cut away the pieces of twine that cross over the top of the box.

You can set the 'tap dancer' in motion in a variety of ways.

Move the end ball-bearing apart from the others and let it go. It will swing down and collide with the others, causing the fifth ball-bearing to be pushed into the air. This, in turn, will swing down and hit the others, and the first one will be pushed out to the side again, and so on.

Next time move the first two ball-bearings out to the side and let them go. The last two will now shoot off because of the force of the impact.

When you do it with three, the centre one will change sides each time to even up the weight.

The movement of the ball-bearings will continue for some time, as the impact of each swing will set off another swing at the other end of the line.

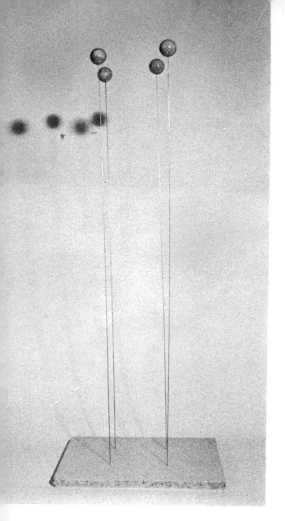

Swaying antennae
You need:
4 ping-pong balls
4 lengths of medium gauge
  piano wire 30 cm. (or
  3 ft.) long (from craft
  shops)
glue
hammer
pincers
1 panel pin (or small nail)
a block of wood
enamel paint

1 Make four holes in the wooden block with the panel pin, removing the pin each time with the pincers.

2 Glue a piece of wire into each of the holes.

3 Put a dab of glue on top of each wire. Push each one through a ping-pong ball until it touches the far side of the ball.

4 Carefully paint the balls and the base.

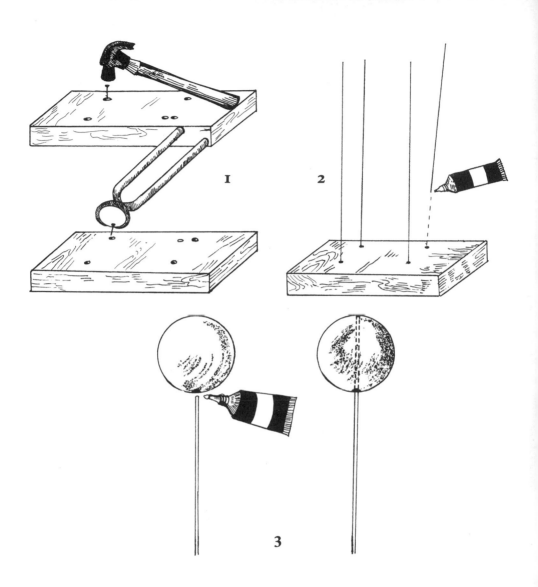

1

2

3

Once the glue has set you will be able to start the antennae swaying through the air. You may like to put them outside the house—in a window-box, perhaps—so that they will move in the wind. Try out different objects on the ends of the wire, and try changing the length of the wires to alter their sway.

Cresta run

You need:
a large piece of corkboard
narrow strips of square
   balsa wood
clear plastic tubing
small nails
elastic bands
small bells
paper, drawing-pins
string, balsa cement
bright coloured paints
small ball-bearings
scissors, hammer
dressmaking pins
several small corks
2 small boxes

1 Decorate the board with a pattern of bright colours. Prop up one end with two or three books to make it slope down.

2 Cement a rim of balsa strips along the edges of the board. Cement more strips across the board to form the runners for the ball-bearings. Make sure they slope just enough to let the balls run slowly down (see diagram on page 53). When the balls reach the far end of each run they must be able to drop onto another piece of wood to take them back across the board (see page 53).

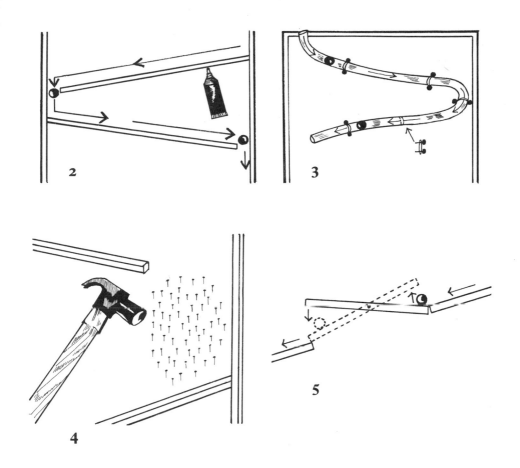

3 Attach the plastic tubing to the board by pinning loops of string across it. The tubing should curve gently downwards as shown in the diagram.

4 Hammer a 'forest of nails' into the corkboard between two of the balsa runs. Each nail should be far enough away from the next to allow the ball-bearings to pass between them.

5 Make a see-saw for the balls by pinning a length of balsa loosely to the board so that the balls run up its gentle slope until their weight tips the balance.

53

These gracefully swaying antennae are surprisingly simple to make (see
page 48)

6 Glue a small box to the board so that its top edge lies directly above the path the ball-bearings will take. Attach a row of bells to this edge using string and drawing-pins. (Diagram 6a shows the side view of the box and 6b the front view.) The bells should hang low enough for the balls to hit them as they pass.

7 Make some tunnels out of rolled paper and cut out little windows so that you can watch the balls pass through them. Position them with drawing-pins.

8 Hammer two nails beneath the end of one of the runs and stretch some elastic bands between them. The ball-bearings will then be able to drop onto the rubber, bounce off, and land on a later part of the run.

9 Pin several corks next to each other as part of the ball-bearings' run.

10 Attach a small, open box to the bottom of the board with drawing-pins. The ball-bearings should drop into it at the end of their run.

Once you have built the 'cresta run' you can keep on adding other exciting obstacles and passage-ways. If you make it carefully enough, each ball will take a surprisingly long time to arrive at the end of its journey.

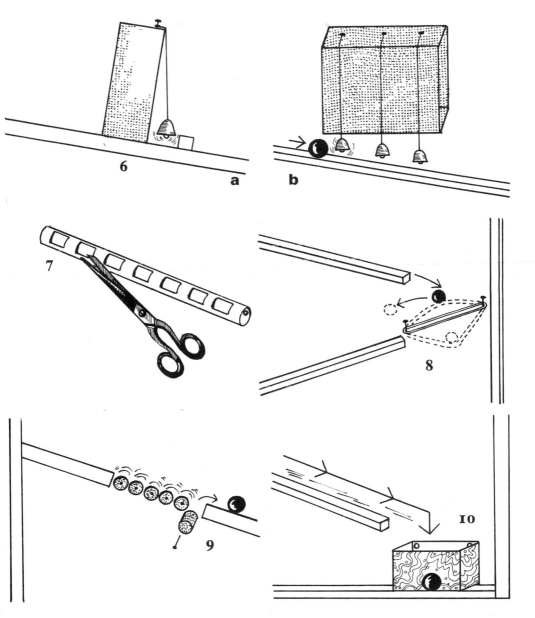

6

a

b

7

8

9

10

Garden orchestra

You need:

a sheet of tin foil about
   1.5 m. (or 5 ft.) long
2 sticks or canes
metal bottle tops
matchsticks
tin cans and an opener
small bells
a metal coat hanger
long nails

an old tennis ball
an old mirror
newspaper
string
cotton
adhesive tape
hammer
glue

56

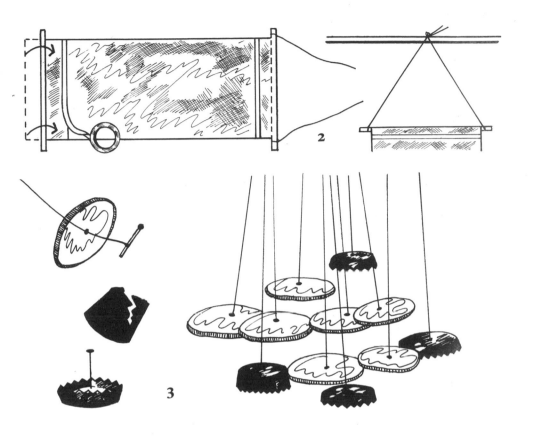

1 Tie a length of string between two trees or posts.

2 Roll the ends of the tin foil round the two sticks and seal them down with adhesive tape. Use strong cotton to tie one of the sticks to the string.

3 Use a hammer and nail to make a hole in the centre of each bottle top. Thread a piece of cotton through each hole and tie it to a piece of matchstick. Hang the bottle tops from the string so that they are almost touching.

4 Tie several small bells to the string with cotton.

5 Remove the ends from some tin cans with the opener. Be careful not to cut your hands. Attach these ends to cotton with adhesive tape (see diagram) and hang them together.

6 Untwist a metal coathanger and bend it into a zigzag. Tie it to the string horizontally and hang up some long nails so that they reach down to the metal.

7 Attach a length of string to the ball by sticking adhesive tape round its middle. Wrap the mirror in newspaper and tap it with the hammer to break it into small pieces. Glue the pieces to the ball and hang the ball from the string.

Even in a gentle breeze the 'orchestra' will begin to play, and when the sun shines the mirrors will flash as they reflect its rays. You could add many different sounds to the orchestra by adding bits and pieces from around the house.

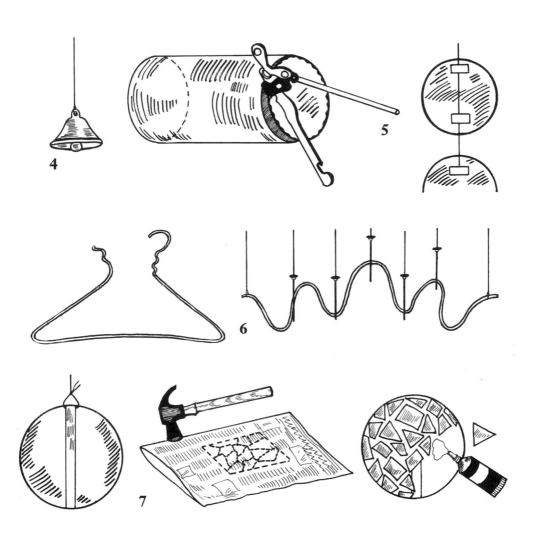

4

5

6

7

Oscillograph

You need:
an empty cocoa tin (or
    similar)
can opener
large balloon
small old mirror
elastic bands
glue
scissors
coloured paper
hammer

1 Remove the bottom of the
cocoa tin with the opener.

2 Cut off the top half of the
balloon and stretch the
remainder over the bottom of
the tin. Keep it in position
with elastic bands.

3 Wrap the mirror in
several layers of newspaper
and tap it with a hammer so
that it breaks into small
pieces. Select one piece
about 1.5 cm. (or $\frac{1}{2}$ in.)
across and put the rest in a
bag for safe keeping. (You
may like to use them to
decorate other kinetics.)

4 Glue the piece of mirror
onto the stretched balloon,
a little away from the centre.

60

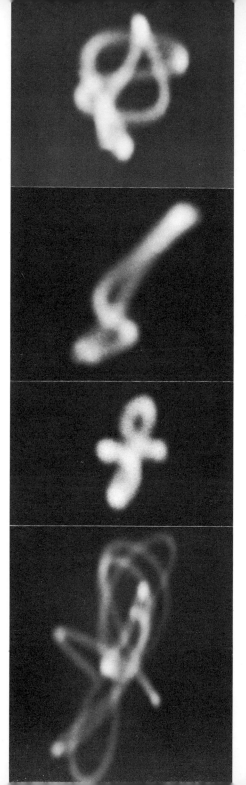

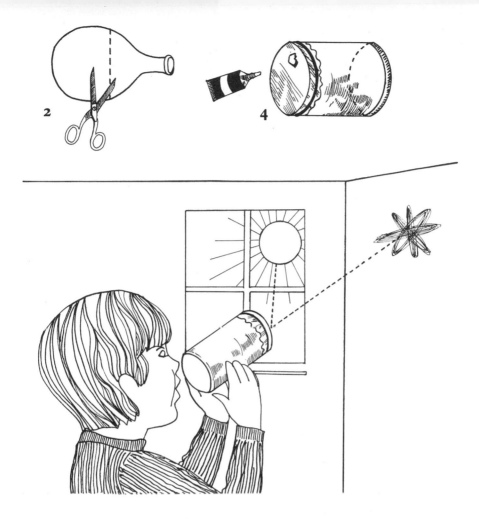

5 Decorate the tin with coloured paper.

You must wait for some sunshine before you can use the 'oscillograph'. Hold it so that the mirror reflects a small patch of sunlight onto a wall. When you make noises into the open end of the tin the sound waves will make the mirror vibrate and a pattern of sound will be seen on the wall. Change the sounds, and different patterns will form. You can put it over the speaker of a record player or radio and watch music being 'drawn' on the wall.

Soft feely box
You need:
a large cardboard box
wire
small plastic bags
cotton wool
a sheet of foam rubber
glue
adhesive tape
scissors
paints or coloured paper

1 Cut a hole in the end of the box large enough for your hand to pass through.

2 Glue the foam rubber to the inside of the box, including the lid. Where the rubber covers the hand-hole, cut two slits in the shape of a cross.

3 Blow up the plastic bags and twist some wire around each opening so that the air does not escape.

4 Arrange the bags in the box and add balls of cotton wool to fill up the spaces.

5 Seal down the lid with adhesive tape and decorate the box with coloured paper or paint.

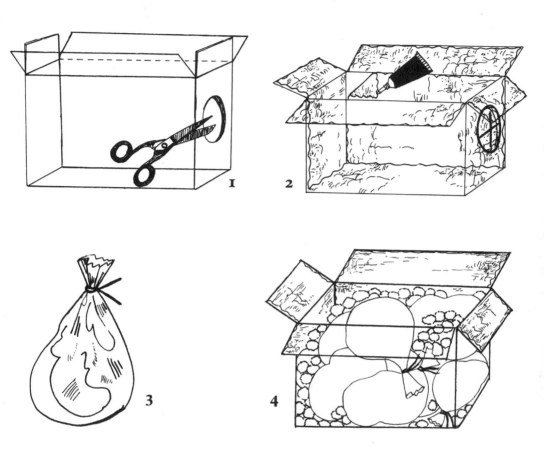

When you put your hand into the box everything you feel will be soft. Give it to your friends to try without telling them what is inside. You could make a whole series of feely boxes, each one having its own special 'feelings'. Use objects like stones, little boxes, and even cornflakes to make a hard feely box, or lots of cotton and elastic bands stretched from side to side for a stringy feely box . . . or whatever you can think of.

More advanced Kinetics

Most of the Kinetics in this book can be made from odds and ends around the house. Once you have made them, you may like to experiment with slightly more sophisticated materials.

Building or construction kits. Have you ever thought how these may be used for making Kinetics? You could, for example, make a Bead Railway.

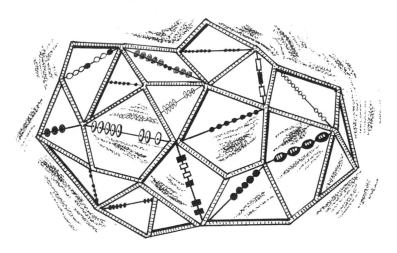

Join together several pieces from your kit to make a large, many-sided shape. Build a criss-cross spider's web inside the area, using fishing line and beads. When you move the shape around, the beads will run along their tracks at all kinds of angles.

Electric or clockwork motors. These are fairly cheap to buy and may be used to power some Kinetics. Used with a construction kit, they can be made to rotate a whole row of coloured patterns (see facing page).

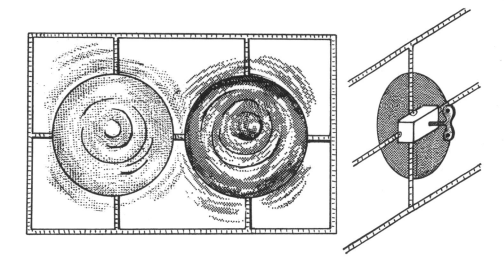

Electro-magnets. You can make one quite easily. All you need is a length of bell-wire (about 1.5 m. or 5 ft.), a large nut and bolt, and a 3-volt battery. Bind two or three layers of wire around the nut and bolt, making sure that each turn of the wire touches the one before. Attach one end of the wire to one terminal of the battery with adhesive tape. Place the other end on the second terminal, and the magnet will be switched on. Stick several pins into a cork and hang it to the ceiling with cotton. If you switch the magnet on and off underneath, the cork will jump about in the air.

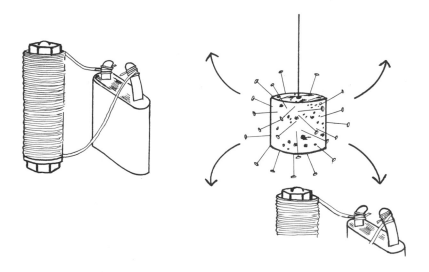

Slide projector. If your family own a projector, ask if you may borrow it to show your own slides. Make some slides on the principle of the light show (page 28) and project the patterns onto a wall or screen.

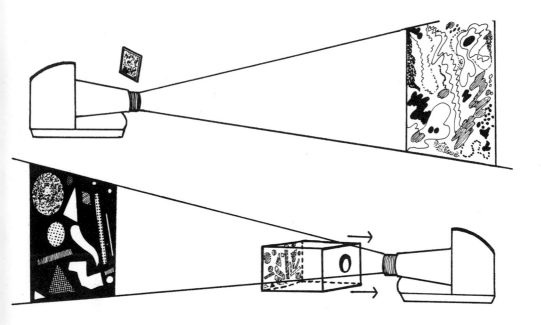

Try cutting a pattern of holes in one end of a cardboard box and cover them with coloured cellophane. Make another hole in the opposite side for the lens and project the pattern.

You could also try projecting the light on other Kinetics—the mobiles, perhaps—and watch the shadows they make; or use mirrors or tin foil to reflect the light at many different angles.

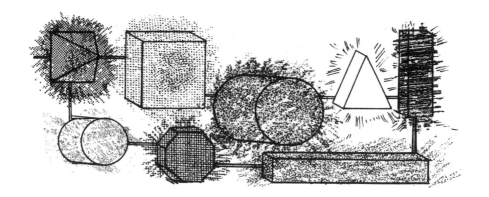

Christmas 'fairy' lights. Pin these up on a wall and cover each light with a fairly large paper shape—use pyramids, cubes, rectangles, and so on—so that the shapes appear to light up when the bulbs are switched on. You can even buy special plugs to make the lights flash on and off. Do not leave the lights switched on while you are out of the room, as there may be a slight fire risk.

Portable hair drier. The current of air from a hair drier can be used to turn windmills. Fold some squares of paper as shown in the photograph. Pin them loosely onto a wall and simply blow air in their direction.

These and many other materials such as springs, fluorescent paint, elastic, cold water dyes, polystyrene and so on make Kinetics a never-ending source of fun and excitement. What ideas do you have?

Index